*The Sayings*

C000000501

*The Sayings of*

# RUDYARD
# KIPLING

edited by

Andrew Rutherford

Duckworth

First published in 1994 by
Gerald Duckworth & Co. Ltd.
The Old Piano Factory
48 Hoxton Square, London N1 6PB
Tel: 071 729 5986
Fax: 071 729 0015

A catalogue record for this book is available
from the British Library

ISBN 0 7156 2621 3

Typeset by Ray Davies
Printed in Great Britain by
Redwood Books, Trowbridge

# Contents

To Nancy

# Introduction

Rudyard Kipling (1865-1936) was for the last decade of the nineteenth century and at least the first two decades of the twentieth the most popular writer in English, in both verse and prose, throughout the English-speaking world. He was the last British author to appeal to readers of all ages, all social classes, and all cultural groups, from lowbrow to highbrow. He was also the last poet to command a mass audience. As a virtuoso in the art of the short story he extended the range of English fiction in both subject-matter and technique; and though some of his later stories are less immediately accessible than his earlier prose works, he did more than any other author – more even than Dickens – to obliterate the division between popular and high art.

His writing tends continually to the aphoristic, and many of his sayings have acquired proverbial status. George Orwell acknowledged, rather reluctantly, in 1942 that Kipling was 'the only English writer of our time who has added phrases to the language', citing instances 'which one sees quoted ... in the gutter press or overhears in saloon bars from people who have barely heard his name': 'East is East and West is West'/'The white man's burden'/'What do they know of England who only England know?'/'The female of the species is more deadly than the male'/'Somewhere East of Suez'/and 'Paying the Danegeld'. It is not surprising that all of these (fragmented and inadequate as they are as samples of Kipling's art) are from his poetry. His prose abounds in terse, knowing, pointed apothegms which approximate at times to epigram, as when (in conversation) he accused newspaper proprietors like Beaverbrook and Rothermere of seeking 'power without responsibility – the prerogative of the harlot throughout the ages' – a phrase which was to be used with telling effect by his cousin Stanley Baldwin, then Prime Minister, in a by-election speech in 1931 (Lord Birkenhead, *Rudyard Kipling*, 1978, p.301; *Times*, 18 March 1931). His fiction, travel-writings and speeches are rich seams yielding nuggets like 'The Japanese is an Oriental, and, therefore, embarrassingly economical of the truth' (*Letters of Travel*, p.51). Or, 'Asia is not going to be civilised after the methods of the West. There is too much Asia and she is too old. You cannot reform a lady of many lovers, and Asia has been insatiable in her flirtations aforetime. She will never attend Sunday school or learn to vote save with swords for tickets' ('The Man Who Was', *Life's Handicap*). Yet his verse is even more pervasively, compulsively quotable – and he has been quoted more frequently than any other modern author – because it is so pithy, so succinct, so unforgettable ('*utterly* and even maddeningly MEMORABLE', as the authors of *1066 and All That* might have said). Which was an effect deliberately sought by Kipling, 'the great object and power of verse' being, as he once told Rider Haggard, 'to put things in a form in which people would not only read but *remember* them'.

Not surprisingly, then, verse quotations predominate in this collection, though prose too is represented and would have bulked larger had space allowed.

From the Boer War onwards many of the intelligentsia turned against Kipling because of his political opinions, and even today he is often dismissed, especially by those who have not read him, as a jingo and imperial propagandist. He was both, unashamedly, at times, yet he cannot be reduced to these simple stereotypes. His thanks to 'Allah who gave me two/Separate sides to my head' point to contradictions or tensions, often fruitful in artistic terms, in his beliefs and character. He sings the praises of both art and action, but throughout his life remains ambivalent about their respective value. Committed, like his own McAndrew, to Law, Order, Duty and Restraint, Obedience, Discipline, he nevertheless feels imaginative sympathy for law-breakers and rebels like Stalky and Co. conspiring against unpopular masters, soldiers and sailors on the spree, or outlaws on the North-West Frontier. He hails the English as a chosen people, but denounces them like an Old Testament prophet for their backslidings and decadence. His vision of Empire is central to much of his finest work, yet in his youth he was an *enfant terrible* of the Raj, mocking official folly and offering comic-satiric sketches as often as serious portrayals of Anglo-Indian life; while in his maturity his pride in British imperial endeavour coexists with an anthropological sense of the validity of other, alternative cultures, with a sense too of the impermanence of all human achievement. He became in many ways an Establishment figure – a personal friend, for example, of George V, for whom he scripted Christmas Day radio addresses to the Empire; yet his greatest originality lay, as Craig Raine observes, in 'the discovery for literature of the underdog' – in his serving as spokesman for the Sons of Martha who do the work of the world, for humble craftsmen, for private soldiers, for Indian peasants, for deep-sea fishermen, for all sorts and conditions of ordinary men.

No single philosophy, therefore, can be extracted from his 'Sayings', the more so as he does not always write *in propria persona*. Rejoicing as he does in the diversity of human creatures, he is drawn to the dramatic lyric or dramatic monologue with their fictional narrators, like the drop-outs in 'Gentlemen-Rankers' or 'The Prodigal Son', the ship's engineer in 'McAndrew's Hymn', the unscrupulous self-made millionaire of 'The "Mary Gloster" ', the Other

Ranks *personae* of *Barrack-Room Ballads*, and hundreds
more, all revealing to the reader their own distinctive
philosophies of and attitudes to life.

The tone of his sayings is as varied as the speakers: it
can be flippant, cynical, humorous, profoundly serious,
mordant, exuberant, stoical or – as it often is – highly
emotional, for he is capable of great intensities of grief,
anger and contempt, not least when writing in his own
person. His art is not confessional, but neither is he an
invisible author. Both his grandfathers had been
Methodist preachers, and he often figures as a preacher
too, urging his secular doctrines with deep, passionate
conviction. He was also a prophet, but as his popularity
waned in later years his denunciations of folly and error
went largely unheeded, and his prophecies, like
Cassandra's, were fated to be disbelieved, though, like
Cassandra's, they had an uncomfortable knack of
coming true.

## Sources and References

The quotations in the Introduction, other than those
from Kipling's own works, are from George Orwell,
*Critical Essays*, 1946, p.109; W.C. Sellar and R.S. Yeatman,
*1066 and All That*, 1930, p.62; Morton Cohen, ed., *Rudyard
Kipling to Rider Haggard: The Record of a Friendship*, 1965,
p.102; and Craig Raine, ed., *Rudyard Kipling: Selected
Poetry*, 1992, p.xi. Unless otherwise noted, all works cited
throughout were published in London.

Verse quotations are identified by the titles of the
poems themselves and the titles, full or abbreviated, of
the volumes in which they were collected. The texts are
from the self-styled 'Definitive Edition' of Kipling's
Verse, though it hardly merits that title as it is far from
being complete, and the contents are arranged
idiosyncratically and unhelpfully. Where poem titles –
e.g. of chapter headings – have not been provided by the
Definitive Edition, information is supplied from the

original collections. Prose quotations are identified by the titles of the stories and those, full or abbreviated, of the volumes in which they were collected; while in the case of Kipling's posthumously published autobiography, *Something of Myself* (1937), his speeches in *A Book of Words* (1928), and his collections of travel writing, *From Sea to Sea and Other Sketches* (1900) and *Letters of Travel: 1892-1913* (1920), page references are given. The texts are from the Uniform Edition.

*Abbreviations*: *DD* (*Departmental Ditties and Other Verses*, 1st and 2nd edns. 1886, 3rd edn. 1888, 4th – and 1st English – edn. 1890); *BRB* (*Barrack-Room Ballads and Other Verses*, 1892); *SS* (*The Seven Seas*, 1896); *FN* (*The Five Nations*, 1903); *YB* (*The Years Between*, 1919); *DE* (*Rudyard Kipling's Verse: Definitive Edition*, 1941); *Plain Tales* (*Plain Tales from the Hills*, 1888); *Puck* (*Puck of Pook's Hill*, 1906), *School History* (*A School History of England*, by C.R.L. Fletcher and Rudyard Kipling, Oxford, 1911).

Other works quoted from include *The Story of the Gadsbys* and *Under the Deodars* (both 1888), *Life's Handicap* (1891), *The Naulahka* (1892), *Many Inventions* (1893), *The Second Jungle Book* (1895), *The Day's Work* (1898), *Kim* (1901), *Just So Stories* (1902), *Traffics and Discoveries* (1904), *Actions and Reactions* (1909), *Rewards and Fairies* (1910), *A Diversity of Creatures* (1917), *Land and Sea Tales for Scouts and Guides* (1923), *Debits and Credits* (1926), and successive 'Inclusive Editions' of the *Verse*.

# Art & Letters

There is pleasure in the wet, wet clay,
When the artist's hand is potting it.
There is pleasure in the wet, wet lay,
When the poet's pad is blotting it.
There is pleasure in the shine of your picture on the line
At the Royal Acade-my;
But the pleasure felt in these is as chalk to Cheddar
        cheese
When it comes to a well-made Lie. –
To a quite unwreckable Lie,
To a most impeccable Lie!
To a water-tight, fire-proof, angle-iron, sunk-hinge,
        time-lock, steel-faced Lie!
Not a private hansom Lie,
But a pair-and-brougham Lie,
Not a little-place-at-Tooting, but a
        country-house-with-shooting
And a ring-fence-deer-park Lie.

        Chapter Heading, *The Naulahka*


When the flush of a new-born sun fell first on Eden's
        green and gold,
Our father Adam sat under the Tree and scratched with
        a stick in the mould;
And the first rude sketch that the world had seen was
        joy to his mighty heart,
Till the Devil whispered behind the leaves, 'It's pretty,
        but is it Art?'

        'The Conundrum of the Workshops', *BRB*


There are nine and sixty ways of constructing tribal lays,
    And every single one of them is right.

        'In the Neolithic Age', *SS*

And the tunes that mean so much to you alone –
   Common tunes that make you choke and blow your
      nose –
Vulgar tunes that bring the laugh that brings the groan –
I can rip your very heartstrings out with those.

'The Song of the Banjo', *SS*

When 'Omer smote 'is bloomin' lyre,
   He'd 'eard men sing by land and sea;
An' what he thought 'e might require,
   'E went an' took – the same as me!

'Introduction to the Barrack-Room
Ballads in *The Seven Seas*'

Fair held the breeze behind us – 'twas warm with lovers'
      prayers.
We'd stolen wills for ballast and a crew of missing heirs.
They shipped as Able Bastards till the Wicked Nurse
      confessed,
And they worked the old three-decker to the Islands of
      the Blest ....

We asked no social questions – we pumped no hidden
      shame –
We never talked obstetrics when the Little Stranger came:
We left the Lord in Heaven, we left the fiends in Hell.
We weren't exactly Yussufs, but – Zuleika didn't tell.

No moral doubt assailed us, so when the port we neared,
The villain had his flogging at the gangway, and we
      cheered.
'Twas fiddle in the foc's'le – 'twas garlands on the mast,
For every one got married, and I went ashore at last.

I left 'em all in couples a-kissing on the decks.
I left the lovers loving and the parents signing cheques.
In endless English comfort, by county-folk caressed,
I left the old three-decker at the Islands of the Blest!

'The Three-Decker' ('*The three-volume novel is extinct*'), *SS*

Romance! Those first-class passengers they like it very
        well,
Printed, an' bound in little books; but why don't poets
        tell?
I'm sick of all their quirks an' turns – the loves an' doves
        they dream –
Lord, send a man like Robbie Burns to sing the Song o'
        Steam!

                'McAndrew's Hymn', *SS*


'Farewell, Romance!' the Cave-men said;
   'With bone well carved He went away.
Flint arms the ignoble arrowhead,
   And jasper tips the spear today.
Changed are the Gods of Hunt and Dance,
And He with these. Farewell, Romance!' ...

'Goodbye Romance!' the Skipper said;
   'He vanished with the coal we burn.
Our dial marks full steam ahead,
   Our speed is timed to half a turn.
Sure as the ferried barge we ply
'Twixt port and port. Romance, goodbye!'

'Romance!' the season-tickets mourn,
   '*He* never ran to catch His train,
But passed with coach and guard and horn –
   And left the local – late again!
Confound Romance!' ... And all unseen
Romance brought up the nine-fifteen.

                'The King', *SS*


When Earth's last picture is painted and the tubes are
        twisted and dried,
When the oldest colours have faded, and the youngest
        critic has died,
We shall rest, and, faith, we shall need it – lie down for
        an aeon or two,
Till the Master of All Good Workmen shall put us to
        work anew ...

And only The Master shall praise us, and only The
　　　Master shall blame,
And no one shall work for money, and no one shall
　　　work for fame,
But each for the joy of the working, and each, in his
　　　separate star,
Shall draw the Thing as he sees It for the God of Things
　　　as They are!

'L'Envoi to *The Seven Seas*'

Much I owe to the Lands that grew –
More to the Lives that fed –
But most to Allah who gave me two
Separate sides to my head.

'The Two-Sided Man', Chapter Heading, *Kim*

If you cross-examine a child of seven or eight on his
day's doings (specially when he wants to go to sleep) he
will contradict himself very satisfactorily. If each
contradiction be set down as a lie and retailed at
breakfast, life is not easy. I have known a certain amount
of bullying, but this was calculated torture .... Yet it
made me give attention to the lies I soon found it
necessary to tell: and this, I presume, is the foundation of
literary effort.

*Something of Myself,* p.6

I was almost nightly responsible for my output to visible
and often brutally voluble critics at the Club [at Lahore].
They were not concerned with my dreams. They wanted
accuracy and interest, but first of all accuracy.

*Ibid,* p.205

And in that Club and elsewhere I met none except
picked men at their definite work – Civilians, Army,
Education, Canals, Forestry, Engineering, Irrigation,
Railways, Doctors, and Lawyers – samples of each
branch and each talking his own shop. It follows then
that that 'show of technical knowledge' for which I was
blamed later came to me from the horse's mouth, even to
boredom. *Ibid,* p.43

I knew a case once. But that is another story.

'False Dawn', *Plain Tales*

They were originally much longer than when they appeared, but the shortening of them, first to my own fancy after rapturous re-readings, and next to the space available, taught me that a tale from which pieces have been raked out is like a fire that has been poked. One does not know that the operation has been performed, but every one feels the effect.

*Something of Myself*, p. 207 (on his early stories)

This leads me to the Higher Editing. Take of well-ground Indian Ink as much as suffices and a camel-hair brush proportionate to the inter-spaces of your lines. In an auspicious hour, read your final draft and consider faithfully every paragraph, sentence and word, blacking out where requisite. Let it lie by to drain as long as possible. At the end of that time, re-read and you should find that it will bear a second shortening. Finally, read it aloud alone and at leisure. Maybe a shade more brushwork will then indicate or impose itself. If not, praise Allah and let it go, and 'when thou hast done, repent not'.

*Ibid*, pp. 207-8

Let us now consider the Personal Daemon of Aristotle and others, of whom it has been truthfully written ...:-
    This is the doom of the Makers – their Daemon lives
            in their pen.
    If he be absent or sleeping, they are even as other
            men ...
Mine came to me early when I sat bewildered among other notions, and said: 'Take this and no other.' I obeyed and was rewarded ... After that I learned to lean on him and recognise the sign of his approach.

*Ibid*, pp. 208-9

My Daemon was with me in the *Jungle Books*, *Kim*, and both Puck books, and good care I took to walk delicately, lest he should withdraw. I know that he did not, because when these books were finished they said so themselves with, almost, the water-hammer click of a tap turned off.

*Ibid*, p.210

Yet, since the tales had to be read by children, before people realised that they were meant for grown-ups; and since they had to be a sort of balance to, as well as a seal upon, some aspects of my 'Imperialistic' output in the past, I worked the material in three or four overlaid tints and textures, which might or might not reveal themselves according to the shifting light of sex, youth, and experience. It was like working lacquer and mother o' pearl, a natural combination, into the same scheme as niello and grisaille, and trying not to let the joins show.
*Something of Myself*, p. 190 (on *Rewards and Fairies*)

There was moreover the old Law: 'As soon as you find you can do anything, do something you can't.'
*Ibid*, p. 190

The Lamp of our Youth will be utterly out, but we shall subsist on the smell of it;
And whatever we do we shall fold our hands and suck our gums and think well of it.
Yes, we shall be perfectly pleased with our work, and that is the Perfectest Hell of it.
'The Old Men', *FN*

C– taught me to loathe Horace for two years; to forget him for twenty, and then to love him for the rest of my days and through many sleepless nights.
*Something of Myself*, p. 33

We have progressed in many directions ... but, so far, we do not seem to have found a sufficient substitute for the necessary word as the final record to which all achievement must look. Even today, when all is done, those who have done it must wait until all has been said by the masterless man with the words ... The Record of the Tribe is its enduring literature.
'Literature', *A Book of Words*, pp. 4–5

Fiction is Truth's elder sister. Obviously. No one in the world knew what truth was till somebody had told a story.
'Fiction', *A Book of Words*, p. 282

… I gave ['Recessional'] to *The Times*. I say 'gave' because for this kind of work I did not take payment. It does not much matter what people think of a man after his death, but I should not like the people whose good opinion I valued to believe that I took money for verses on Joseph Chamberlain, Rhodes, Lord Milner, or any of my South African verse in *The Times*.

*Ibid*, p. 148

When I was a King and a Mason – a Master proven and
      skilled –
I cleared me ground for a Palace such as a King should
      build,
I decreed and dug down to my levels. Presently, under
      the silt,
I came on the wreck of a Palace such as a King had built.

There was no worth in the fashion – there was no wit in
      the plan –
Hither and thither, aimless, the ruined footings ran –
Masonry, brute, mishandled, but carven on every stone:
'*After me cometh a Builder. Tell him, I too have known*' …

When I was a King and a Mason – in the open noon of
      my pride,
They sent me a Word from the Darkness. They
      whispered and called me aside.
They said – 'The end is forbidden.' They said –'Thy use
      is fulfilled.
Thy Palace shall stand as that other's – the spoil of a
      King who shall build'.
I called my men from my trenches, my quarries, my
      wharves, and my sheers.
All I had wrought I abandoned to the faith of the
      faithless years.
Only I cut on the timber – only I carved on the stone:
'*After me cometh a Builder. Tell him, I too have known!*'

'The Palace', *FN*

I reckon there's more things told than are true,
And more things true than are told!

'The Ballad of Minepit Shaw', *Rewards and Fairies*

Ah! What avails the classic bent
    And what the cultured word,
Against the undoctored incident
    That actually occurred?

And what is Art whereto we press
    Through paint and prose and rhyme –
When Nature in her nakedness
    Defeats us every time?

'The Benefactors', Heading from *A Diversity of Creatures*
('The Edge of the Evening')

Once, after long-drawn revel at The Mermaid,
He to the overbearing Boanerges
Jonson, uttered (if half of it were liquor,
    Blessed be the vintage!)

Saying how, at an alehouse under Cotswold,
He had made sure of his very Cleopatra
Drunk with enormous, salvation-contemning
    Love for a tinker.

How, while he hid from Sir Thomas's keepers,
Crouched in a ditch and drenched by the midnight
Dews, he had listened to gipsy Juliet
    Rail at the dawning.

How at Bankside, a boy drowning kittens
Winced at the business; whereupon his sister –
Lady Macbeth aged seven – thrust 'em under,
    Sombrely scornful.

'The Craftsman', *YB*

What boots it on the Gods to call?
    Since, answered or unheard,
We perish with the Gods and all
    Things made – except the Word …

Yet they who use the Word assigned,
    To hearten and make whole,
Not less than Gods have served mankind,
    Though vultures rend their soul.

'A Recantation', *YB*

... the 'Higher Cannibalism' in biography ... the
exhumation of scarcely cold notorieties, defenceless
females for choice, and tricking them out with sprightly
inferences and 'sex' deductions to suit the mood of the
market.

*Something of Myself*, pp. 191-2

If I have given you delight
  By aught that I have done,
Let me lie quiet in that night
  Which shall be yours anon:

And for the little, little, span
  The dead are borne in mind,
Seek not to question other than
  The books I leave behind.

'The Appeal', *DE*

# Women & Love

Two things greater than all things are,
The first is Love, and the second War.
And since we know not how War may prove,
Heart of my heart, let us talk of Love!
'The Ballad of the King's Jest', BRB

Down to Gehenna or up to the Throne
He travels the fastest who travels alone.

White hands cling to the tightened rein,
    Slipping the spur from the booted heel,
Tenderest voices cry, 'Turn again!'
    Red lips tarnish the scabbarded steel,
High hopes faint on a warm hearth-stone –
He travels the fastest who travels alone.
'The Winners', 'L'Envoi' to The Story of the Gadsbys (Soldiers Three)

'They are fools who kiss and tell' –
    Wisely has the poet sung.
Man may hold all sorts of posts
    If he'll only hold his tongue.
'Pink Dominoes', DD

Who are the rulers of Ind – to whom shall we bow the
            knee?
Make your peace with the women, and men will make
            you L.G. [Lieutenant-Governor]
'Certain Maxims of Hafiz,' DD

Pleasant the snaffle of Courtship, improving the
            manners and carriage;
But the colt who is wise will abstain from the terrible
            thorn-bit of Marriage.
Ibid

My Son, if a maiden deny thee and scufflingly bid thee
      give o'er,
Yet lip meets with lip at the lastward. Get out! She has
      been there before.
They are pecked on the ear and the chin and the nose
      who are lacking in lore. *Ibid*


A woman is only a woman, but a good Cigar is a Smoke.
  'The Betrothed' ('*You must choose between me and your cigar*'), *DD*


Excepting, always, falling off a horse there is nothing
more fatally easy than marriage before the Registrar.
        'In the Pride of His Youth', *Plain Tales*


Perhaps … he gave way to the queer savage feeling that
sometimes takes by the throat a husband twenty years
married, when he sees, across the table, the same, same
face of his wedded wife, and knows that, as he has sat
facing it, so must he continue to sit until the day of its
death or his own. Most men and all women know the
spasm.
        'The Bronkhorst Divorce Case', *Plain Tales*


'Take my word for it, the silliest woman can manage a
clever man; but it needs a very clever woman to manage
a fool.'    Mrs Hauksbee in 'Three and – An Extra', *Plain Tales*


Never praise a sister to a sister, in the hope of your
compliments reaching the proper ears, and so preparing
the way for you later on. Sisters are women first, and
sisters afterwards …
        'False Dawn', *Plain Tales*


'[She said] that being kissed by a man who *didn't* wax his
moustache was – like eating an egg without salt.'
        *The Story of the Gadsbys (Soldiers Three)*


Once upon a time there was a Man and his Wife and a
Tertium Quid. All three were unwise, but the Wife was
the unwisest.
    'At the Pit's Mouth', *Under the Deodars (Wee Willie Winkie)*


For the sin ye do by two and two ye must pay for one by
      one!        'Tomlinson', *BRB*

The sins o' four an' forty years, all up an' down the seas,
Clack an' repeat like valves half-fed … Forgie's our
        trespasses! …
Years when I raked the Ports wi' pride to fill my cup o'
        wrong –
Judge not, O Lord, my steps aside at Gay Street in
        Hong-Kong!
Blot out the wastrel hours of mine in sin when I abode –
Jane Harrigan's an' Number Nine, The Reddick an'
        Grant Road!

                    'McAndrew's Hymn', *SS*


Till, off Sambawa Head, Ye mind, I heard a land-breeze
        ca',
Milk-warm wi' breath o' spice an' bloom: 'McAndrew,
        come awa'! …
Your mither's God's a graspin' deil, the shadow o'
        yoursel',
Got out o' books by meenisters clean daft on Heaven an'
        Hell.
They mak' him in the Broomielaw, o' Glasgie cold an'
        dirt,
A jealous, pridefu' fetish, lad, that's only strong to hurt.
Ye'll not go back to Him again an' kiss His red-hot rod,
But come wi' Us' (Now, who were *They*?) 'an' know the
        Leevin' God,
That does not kipper souls for sport or break a life in jest,
But swells the ripenin' cocoanuts an' ripes the woman's
        breast.'

                    *Ibid*


Now if you must marry, take care she is old –
A troop-sergeant's widow's the nicest, I'm told,
For beauty won't help if your rations is cold,
   Nor love ain't enough for a soldier ….

If the wife should go wrong with a comrade, be loth
To shoot when you catch 'em – you'll swing, on my
        oath! –
Make 'im take 'er and keep 'er: that's Hell for them both,
   An' you're shut o' the curse of a soldier.

              'The Young British Soldier,' *BRB*

I am sick o' wastin' leather on these gritty pavin'-stones,
An' the blasted English drizzle wakes the fever in my
      bones;
Tho' I walks with fifty 'ousemaids outer Chelsea to the
      Strand,
An' they talks a lot o' lovin', but wot do they
      understand?
  Beefy face an' grubby 'and –
  Law! wot do they understand?
  I've a neater, sweeter maiden in a cleaner, greener
      land!
  On the road to Mandalay ...

                      'Mandalay', *BRB*


'E was warned agin' 'er –
  That's what made him look:
She was warned agin' 'im –
  That is why she took ...

Now it's done an' over,
  'Ear the organ squeak,
'*Voice that breathed o'er Eden*' –
  Ain't she got the cheek!
White an' laylock ribbons,
  'Think yourself so fine!
I'd pray God to take yer
  'Fore I made you mine! ...

Bowin' like a lady,
  Blushin' like a lad –
'Oo would say to see 'em
  Both is rotten bad?

             'The Sergeant's Weddin'', *SS*

*Now I aren't no 'and with the ladies,*
  *For, taking 'em all along,*
*You never can say till you've tried 'em,*
  *An' then you are like to be wrong.*
*There's times when you'll think that you mightn't,*
  *There's times when you'll know that you might;*
*But the things you will learn from the Yellow an' Brown,*
  *They'll 'elp you a lot with the White!*

             'The Ladies', *SS*

I was a young 'un at 'Oogli,
  Shy as a girl to begin;
Aggie de Castrer she made me,
  An' Aggie was clever as sin;
Older than me but my first 'un –
  More like a mother she were –
Showed me the way to promotion an' pay,
  An' I learned about women from 'er!

Then I was ordered to Burma,
  Actin' in charge o' Bazar,
An' I got me a tiddy live 'eathen
  Through buyin' supplies off 'er pa.
Funny an' yellow an' faithful –
  Doll in a teacup she were –
But we lived on the square, like a true-married pair.
  An' I learned about women from 'er!

Then we was shifted to Neemuch
  (Or I might ha' been keepin' 'er now),
An' I took with a shiny she-devil,
  The wife of a nigger at Mhow;
Taught me the gipsy-folks *bolee* [slang];
  Kind o' volcano she were,
For she knifed me one night 'cause I wished she was
      white,
  And I learned about women from 'er!

Then I come 'ome in a trooper,
  'Long of a kid o' sixteen –
Girl from a convent at Meerut,
  The straightest I ever 'ave seen.
Love at first sight was 'er trouble,
  *She* didn't know what it were;
An' I wouldn't do such, 'cause I liked 'er too much,
  But – I learned about women from 'er!

I've taken my fun where I've found it,
   An' now I must pay for my fun,
For the more you 'ave known o' the others
   The less will you settle to one;
An' the end of it's sittin' and thinkin',
   An' dreamin' Hell-fires to see;
So be warned by my lot (which I know you will not),
   An' learn about women from me!       *Ibid*

*What did the Colonel's Lady think?*
   *Nobody never knew.*
*Somebody asked the Sergeant's Wife,*
   *An' she told 'em true!*
*When you get to a man in the case,*
   *They're like as a row of pins –*
*For the Colonel's Lady an' Judy O'Grady*
   *Are sisters under their skins!*       *Ibid*

Nice while it lasted, an' now it is over –
Tear out your 'eart an' good-bye to your lover!
What's the use o' grievin', when the mother that bore
        you
(Mary, pity women!) knew it all before you?

When a man is tired there is naught will bind 'im;
All 'e solemn promised 'e will shove be'ind 'im.
What's the good o' prayin' for The Wrath to strike 'im
(Mary, pity women!) when the rest are like 'im?
      ' "Mary, Pity Women!" ' *SS*

The female of the species is more deadly than the male.
      'The Female of the Species', *YB*

A fool there was and he made his prayer
   (Even as you and I!)
To a rag and a bone and a hank of hair
(We called her the woman who did not care)
But the fool he called her his lady fair –
   (Even as you and I!)
      'The Vampire', *Verse : Inclusive Edition,* 1919

'That's the secret. 'Tisn't beauty, so to speak, nor good
talk necessarily. It's just It.'
      'Mrs Bathurst', *Traffics and Discoveries*

What is a woman that you forsake her,
And the hearth-fire and the home-acre,
To go with the old grey Widow-maker?

She has no house to lay a guest in –
But one chill bed for all to rest in,
That the pale suns and the stray bergs nest in.

She has no strong white arms to fold you,
But the ten-times-fingering weed to hold you –
Out on the rocks where the tide has rolled you.

Yet when the signs of summer thicken,
And the ice breaks, and the birch-buds quicken,
Yearly you turn from our side, and sicken –

Sicken again for the shouts and the slaughters.
You steal away to the lapping waters,
And look at your ship in her winter-quarters.

You forget our mirth, and talk at the tables,
The kine in the shed and the horse in the stables –
To pitch her sides and go over her cables.

Then you drive out where the storm-clouds swallow,
And the sound of your oar-blades, falling hollow;
Is all we have left through the months to follow.

Ah, what is Woman that you forsake her,
And the hearth-fire and the home-acre,
To go with the old grey Widow-maker?
                    'Harp Song of the Dane Women', *Puck*

I have slain none except my Mother. She
(Blessing her slayer) died of grief for me.
                    'Epitaphs of the War 1914-18 : An Only Son', *YB*

# England & the English

They [London intellectuals] derided my poor little Gods of the East, and asserted that the British in India spent violent lives 'oppressing' the Native. (This in a land where white girls of sixteen, at twelve or fourteen pounds per annum, hauled thirty or forty pounds weight of bath-water at a time up four flights of stairs!)
*Something of Myself*, p. 91

Mr Silas Riley, Accountant, was a most curious animal – a long, gawky, rawboned Yorkshireman, full of the savage self-conceit that blossoms only in the best county in England. 'A Bank Fraud', *Plain Tales*

In Manchester was a paper called *The Manchester Guardian*. Outside the mule-lines I had never met anything that could kick or squeal so continuously, or so completely round the entire compass of things.
*Something of Myself*, p. 211

We have fed our sea for a thousand years
    And she calls us, still unfed,
Though there's never a wave of all her waves
    But marks our English dead:
We have strawed our best to the weed's unrest,
    To the shark and the sheering gull.
If blood be the price of admiralty,
    Lord God, we ha' paid in full!
'A Song of the English: The Song of the Dead', *SS*

Oh, my country, bless the training that from cot to castle
        runs –
The pitfall of the stranger but the bulwark of thy sons –
Measured speech and ordered action, sluggish soul and
        unperturbed,
Till we wake our Island-Devil – nowise cool for being
        curbed! 'Et Dona Ferentes', *FN*

God gives all men all earth to love,
  But, since man's heart is small,
Ordains for each one spot shall prove
  Belovèd over all.
Each to his choice, and I rejoice
  The lot has fallen to me
In a fair ground – in a fair ground –
  Yea, Sussex by the sea.                    'Sussex', *FN*


I am slowly discovering England which is the most
wonderful foreign land I have ever been in.
                    Letter to H. Rider Haggard, Dec. 1902


Me that 'ave been what I've been –
Me that 'ave gone where I've gone –
Me that 'ave seen what I've seen –
  'Ow can I ever take on
With awful old England again,
An' 'ouses both sides of the street,
And 'edges two sides of the lane,
And the parson an' gentry between,
An' touchin' my 'at when we meet –
  Me that 'ave been what I've been?
      'Chant-Pagan (*English Irregular, discharged*)', *FN*


If England was what England seems,
  An' not the England of our dreams,
But only putty, brass, an' paint,
  'Ow quick we'd drop 'er! *But she ain't*!
                    'The Return (*All Arms*)', *FN*


Sons of the sheltered city – unmade, unhandled, unmeet –
Ye pushed them raw to the battle as ye picked them raw
      from the street ...
And ye vaunted your fathomless power, and ye flaunted
      your iron pride,
Ere – ye fawned on the Younger Nations for the men
      who could shoot and ride!
Then ye returned to your trinkets; then ye contented
      your souls
With the flannelled fools at the wicket or the muddied
      oafs at the goals.
                    'The Islanders', *FN*

Now we can only wait till the day, wait and apportion
        our shame.
These are the dykes our fathers left, but we would not
        look to the same.
Time and again we were warned of the dykes, time and
        again we delayed:
Now, it may fall, we have slain our sons, as our fathers
        we have betrayed.        'The Dykes', *FN*


Trackway and Camp and City lost,
Salt Marsh where now is corn –
Old Wars, old Peace, old Arts that cease,
And so was England born!


She is not any common Earth,
Water or wood or air,
But Merlin's Isle of Gramarye,
Where you and I will fare!        'Puck's Song', *Puck*


Land of our Birth, our faith, our pride,
For whose dear sake our fathers died;
Oh, Motherland, we pledge to thee
Head, heart and hand through the years to be!
       'The Children's Song', *Puck*


Take of English earth as much
As either hand may rightly clutch.
In the taking of it breathe
Prayer for all who lie beneath.
Not the great nor well-bespoke,
But the mere uncounted folk
Of whose life and death is none
Report or lamentation.
    Lay that earth upon thy heart,
    And thy sickness shall depart! …
These shall cleanse and purify
Webbed and inward-turning eye;
These shall show thee treasure hid
Thy familiar fields amid;
And reveal (which is thy need)
Every man a King indeed!
      'A Charm (Introduction to *Rewards and Fairies*)'

'The Saxon is not like us Normans. His manners are not
 so polite.
But he never means anything serious till he talks about
 justice and right.
When he stands like an ox in the furrow with his sullen
 set eyes on your own,
And grumbles, 'This isn't fair dealing', my son, leave the
 Saxon alone.'

       'Norman and Saxon', *School History*


The child of Mary Queen of Scots,
 A shifty mother's shiftless son,
Bred up among intrigues and plots,
 Learned in all things, wise in none …
He was the author of his line –
 He wrote that witches should be burnt;
He wrote that monarchs were divine,
 And left a son who – proved they weren't!
       'James I', *School History*


If wars were won by feasting,
 Or victory by song,
Or safety found in sleeping sound,
 How England would be strong!
But honour and dominion
 Are not maintainèd so.
They've only got by sword and shot,
 *And this the Dutchmen know*!
   'The Dutch in the Medway (1664-72)', *School History*


'Then what can I do for you, all you Big Steamers,
 Oh, what can I do for your comfort and good?'
'Send out your big warships to watch your big waters,
 That no one may stop us from bringing you food.

*For the bread that you eat and the biscuits you nibble,*
 *The sweets that you suck and the joints that you carve,*
*They are brought to you daily by all us Big Steamers –*
 *And if any one hinders our coming you'll starve!'*
      'Big Steamers', *School History*

Our England is a garden, and such gardens are not made
By singing:– 'Oh, how beautiful!' and sitting in the shade,
While better men than we go out and start their working
        lives
At grubbing weeds from gravel-paths with broken
        dinner-knives.
                    'The Glory of the Garden', *School History*


… brittle intellectuals/Who crack beneath a strain –
                                'The Holy War', *YB*


Those Downs moved me to write some verses called
'Sussex'. To-day, from Rottingdean to Newhaven is
almost fully developed suburb, of great horror.
                        *Something of Myself*, p. 137


The Pope may launch his Interdict,
    The Union its decree,
But the bubble is blown and the bubble is pricked
    By Us and such as We.
Remember the battle and stand aside
    While Thrones and Powers confess
That King over all the children of pride
    Is the Press – the Press – the Press!
            'The Press', *A Diversity of Creatures* ('The Village
                            that Voted the Earth was Flat')


When men grew shy of hunting stag,
    For fear the Law might try 'em,
The Car put up an average bag
    Of twenty dead *per diem*.
Then every road was made a rink
    For Coroners to sit on;
And so began, in skid and stink,
    The real blood-sport of Britain!
                'Fox-Hunting (The Fox Meditates)',
                    *Verse: Inclusive Edition*, 1933


This is the midnight – let no star
Delude us – dawn is very far.
This is the tempest long foretold –
Slow to make head but sure to hold.

Stand by! The lull 'twixt blast and blast
Signals the storm is near, not past;
And worse than present jeopardy
May our forlorn tomorrow be ...

It is decreed that we abide
The weight of gale against the tide
And those huge waves the outer main
Sends in to set us back again ...

She moves, with all save purpose lost,
To make her offing from the coast;
But, till she fetches open sea,
Let no man deem that he is free!     'The Storm Cone', *Ibid*


From the date that the doors of his prep-school close
    On the lonely little son
He is taught by precept, insult, and blows
    The Things that Are Never Done ...

Slack by training and slow by birth,
    Only quick to despise,
Largely assessing his neighbour's worth
    By the hue of his socks or ties,
A loafer-in-grain, his foes maintain,
    And how shall we combat their view
When, atop of his natural sloth, he holds
    There are Things no Fellow can do?

'The Waster', *DE*


It is entirely right that the English should mistrust and
disregard all the Arts and most of the Sciences, for on
that indifference rests their moral grandeur, but their
starvation in their estimates is sometimes too marked.
    *Something of Myself*, p. 144

# The Empire

Thus the artless songs I sing
Do not deal with anything
    New or never said before.
As it was in the beginning
Is today official sinning,
    And shall be for evermore!

'General Summary', *DD*

He was out in India for three months collecting materials
for a book on 'Our Eastern Impedimenta', and
quartering himself upon everybody, like a Cossack in
evening-dress.

'The Three Musketeers', *Plain Tales*

Now India is a place beyond all others where one must
not take things too seriously – the mid-day sun always
excepted. Too much work and too much energy kill a
man just as effectively as too much assorted vice or too
much drink.

'Thrown Away', *Plain Tales*

One of the many curses of our life in India is the want of
atmosphere in the painter's sense. There are no half-tints
worth noticing. Men stand out all crude and raw, with
nothing to tone them down, and nothing to scale them
against.

'Wressley of the Foreign Office', *Plain Tales*

Oh, East is East, and West is West, and never the twain
        shall meet.
Till Earth and Sky stand presently at God's great
        Judgment Seat;
But there is neither East nor West, Border, nor Breed, nor
        Birth,
When two strong men stand face to face, though they
        come from the ends of the earth!

'The Ballad of East and West', *BRB*

Bit by bit, my original notion grew into a vast, vague conspectus – Army and Navy Stores List if you like – of the whole sweep and meaning of things and effort and origins throughout the Empire. I visualised it, as I do most ideas, in the shape of a semi-circle of buildings and temples projecting into a sea – of dreams.

*Something of Myself*, p. 91

What should they know of England who only England know?

'The English Flag', *BRB*

Now it is not good for the Christian's health to hustle the
 Aryan brown,
For the Christian riles, and the Aryan smiles and he
 weareth the Christian down;
And the end of the fight is a tombstone white with the
 name of the late deceased,
And the epitaph drear : 'A Fool lies here who tried to
 hustle the East.'

Chapter Heading, *The Naulahka*

Keep ye the Law – be swift in all obedience –
Clear the land of evil, drive the road and bridge the ford.
 Make ye sure to each his own
 That he reap where he hath sown;
By the peace among Our peoples let men know we serve
 the Lord!   'A Song of the English', *SS*

God of our fathers, known of old,
 Lord of our far-flung battle-line,
Beneath whose awful Hand we hold
 Dominion over palm and pine –
Lord God of Hosts, be with us yet,
Lest we forget – lest we forget!

The tumult and the shouting dies;
 The Captains and the Kings depart:
Still stands Thine ancient sacrifice,
 An humble and a contrite heart.
Lord God of Hosts, be with us yet,
Lest we forget – lest we forget!

Far-called, our navies melt away;
    On dune and headland sinks the fire:
Lo, all our pomp of yesterday
    Is one with Nineveh and Tyre!
Judge of the Nations, spare us yet,
Lest we forget – lest we forget!

If, drunk with sight of power, we loose
    Wild tongues that have not Thee in awe,
Such boastings as the Gentiles use,
    Or lesser breeds without the Law –
Lord God of Hosts, be with us yet,
Lest we forget – lest we forget!

For heathen heart that puts her trust
    In reeking tube and iron shard,
All valiant dust that builds on dust,
    And, guarding, calls not Thee to guard,
For frantic boast and foolish word –
Thy mercy on Thy People, Lord!

'Recessional', *FN*


Take up the White Man's burden –
    Send forth the best ye breed –
Go bind your sons to exile
    To serve your captives' need;
To wait in heavy harness
    On fluttered folk and wild –
Your new-caught, sullen peoples,
    Half devil and half child ...

Take up the White Man's burden –
    The savage wars of peace –
Fill full the mouth of Famine
    And bid the sickness cease;
And when your goal is nearest,
    The end for others sought,
Watch Sloth and heathen Folly
    Bring all your hope to nought ...

Take up the White Man's burden –
    And reap his old reward:
The blame of those ye better,
    The hate of those ye guard ...

'The White Man's Burden (*The United States
and the Philippine Islands*)', FN


Who gives him the Bath?
'I,' said the wet,
'Rank Jungle-sweat,
I'll give him the Bath!'

Who'll sing the Psalms?
'We,' said the Palms.
'As the hot wind becalms,
We'll sing the psalms.'

Who lays on the Sword?
'I,' said the Sun,
'Before he has done,
I'll lay on the sword.'

Who fastens his belt?
'I,' said Short-Rations,
'I know all the fashions
Of tightening a belt!'

Who gives him his spur?
'I,' said his Chief,
Exacting and brief,
'I'll give him the spur.'

Who'll shake his hand?
'I,' said the Fever.
'And I'm no deceiver,
I'll shake his hand.'

Who brings him the wine?
'I,' said Quinine,
'It's a habit of mine.
I'll come with his wine.'

Who puts him to proof?
'I,' said All Earth.
'Whatever he's worth,
I'll put to the proof ...'

'The New Knighthood', Actions and<br>Reactions ('A Deal in Cotton')

'There's no sense in going further – it's the edge of
　　　cultivation',
　　So they said, and I believed it – broke my land and
　　　　sowed my crop –
Built my farms and strung my fences in the little border
　　　station
　　Tucked away below the foothills where the trails run
　　　　out and stop:

Till a voice, as bad as Conscience, rang interminable
　　　changes
　　On one everlasting Whisper day and night repeated –
　　　　so:
'Something hidden. Go and find it. Go and look behind
　　　the Ranges –
　　Something lost behind the Ranges. Lost and waiting
　　　　for you. Go!'

'The Explorer', FN

I charge you charge your glasses –
　　I charge you drink with me
To the men of the Four New Nations,
　　And the Islands of the Sea ...

'The Native-Born', SS

*Let us admit it fairly, as a business people should,*
*We have had no end of a lesson: it will do us no end of good ...*

It was our fault, and our very great fault – and now we
　　　must turn it to use.
We have forty million reasons for failure, but not a
　　　single excuse.
So the more we work and the less we talk the better
　　　result we shall get.
We have had an Imperial lesson. It may make us an
　　　Empire yet!

'The Lesson 1899-1902 (Boer War)', FN

At long last, we were left apologising to a deeply indignant people [the Boers], whom we had been nursing and doctoring for a year or two ... We put them in a position to uphold and expand their primitive lust for racial domination, and thanked God we were 'rid of a knave'.
*Something of Myself*, p. 166

The men of my own stock,
    They may do ill or well,
But they tell the lies I am wonted to,
    They are used to the lies I tell;
And we do not need interpreters
    When we go to buy and sell.

The Stranger within my gates,
    He may be evil or good.
But I cannot tell what powers control –
    What reasons sway his mood;
Nor when the Gods of his far-off land
    Shall repossess his blood.

The men of my own stock.
    Bitter bad they may be,
But, at least, they hear the things I hear,
    And see the things I see;
And whatever I think of them and their likes
    They think of the likes of me.
'The Stranger (Canadian)', *Letters of Travel*
(Canadian edn.), *Songs from Books*.

O ye who tread the Narrow Way
    By Tophet-flare to Judgment Day,
Be gentle when 'the heathen' pray
    To Buddha at Kamakura!
'Buddha at Kamakura', *FN* (from Chapter Heading, *Kim*)

'Blessèd be the English and all their ways and works.
Cursèd be the Infidels, Hereticks and Turks!'
'Amen', quo' Jobson, 'but where I used to lie
Was neither Candle, Bell nor Book to curse my brethren
        by,

But a palm-tree in full bearing, bowing down, bowing
                    down,
To a surf that drove unsparing at the brown, walled
                    town –
Conches in a temple, oil-lamps in a dome –
And a low moon out of Africa said: "This way home!" '

'Blessèd be the English and all that they profess.
Cursèd be the Savages that prance in nakedness!'
'Amen', quo' Jobson, 'but where I used to lie
Was neither shirt nor pantaloons to catch my brethren
                    by:

But a well-wheel slowly creaking, going round, going
                    round,
By a water-channel leaking over drowned, warm ground –
Parrots very busy in the trellised pepper-vine –
And a high sun over Asia shouting: "Rise and shine!" '
                              'Jobson's Amen', *A Diversity of*
                              *Creatures* ('In the Presence')

Father, Mother, and Me,
    Sister and Auntie say
All the people like us are We,
    And every one else is They.
And They live over the sea,
    While We live over the way,
But – would you believe it? – They look upon We
    As only a sort of They!
                          'We and They', *Debits and Credits*
                          ('A Friend of the Family')

We hold today one square mile in every four of the land
of the globe, and through our representatives we are
responsible for the protection of one person in five out of
the entire population of this little planet.
        'The Ritual of Government', *A Book of Words*, pp. 67-8

Cities and Thrones and Powers
    Stand in Time's eye,
Almost as long as flowers,
    Which daily die ...    'Cities and Thrones and Powers', *Puck*
                          ('A Centurion of the Thirtieth')

# Wars & Soldiering

A great and glorious thing it is
    To learn, for seven years or so,
The Lord knows what of that and this,
    Ere reckoned fit to face the foe –
The flying bullet down the Pass,
That whistles clear: 'All flesh is grass.' ...

A scrimmage in a Border Station –
    A canter down some dark defile –
Two thousand pounds of education
    Drops to a ten-rupee jezail –
The Crammer's boast, the Squadron's pride,
Shot like a rabbit in a ride!

No proposition Euclid wrote,
    No formulae the text-books know,
Will turn the bullet from your coat,
    Or ward the tulwar's downward blow.
Strike hard who cares – shoot straight who can –
The odds are on the cheaper man.

'Arithmetic on the Frontier', *DD*


'Ave you 'eard 'o the Widow at Windsor
    With a hairy gold crown on 'er 'ead?
She 'as ships on the foam – she 'as millions at 'ome,
    An' she pays us poor beggars in red ...

Walk wide o' the Widow at Windsor,
    For 'alf o' Creation she owns:
We 'ave bought 'er the same with the sword an' the
            flame,
    An' we've salted it down with our bones.
            (Poor beggars! – it's blue with our bones!)

Hands off o' the sons o' the Widow,
   Hands off o' the goods in 'er shop,
For the Kings must come down an' the Emperors frown
   When the Widow at Windsor says 'Stop!'
            (Poor beggars! – we're sent to say 'Stop!')
                        'The Widow at Windsor', *BRB*


'Where have you been this while away,
               Johnnie, Johnnie?'
Out with the rest on a picnic lay ...
They called us out of the barrack-yard
To Gawd knows where from Gosport Hard,
And you can't refuse when you get the card,
   And the Widow gives the party ...

'What ha' you done with half your mess,
               Johnnie, Johnnie?'
They couldn't do more and they wouldn't do less ...
They ate their whack and they drank their fill,
And I think the rations has made them ill,
For half my comp'ny's lying still
   Where the Widow give the party ...

'What was the end of all the show,
               Johnnie, Johnnie?'
Ask my Colonel, for I don't know ...
We broke a King and we built a road –
A court-house stands where the Reg'ment goed.
And the river's clean where the raw blood flowed
   When the Widow give the party.
                        'The Widow's Party', *BRB*


First mind you steer clear o' the grog-sellers' huts,
For they sell you Fixed Bay'nets that rots out your guts –
Ay, drink that 'ud eat the live steel from your butts –
   An' it's bad for the young British soldier ...

When first under fire an' you're wishful to duck
Don't look nor take 'eed at the man that is struck.
Be thankful you're livin' an' trust to your luck
   And march to your front like a soldier ...

If your officer's dead and the sergeants look white,
Remember it's ruin to run from a fight:
So take open order, lie down, and sit tight,
    And wait for supports like a soldier ...

When you're wounded and left on Afghanistan's plains,
And the women come out to cut up what remains,
Jest roll to your rifle and blow out your brains
    An' go to your Gawd like a soldier.

              'The Young British Soldier', *BRB*

The moril of this story, it is plainly to be seen:
You 'aven't got no families when servin' of the Queen –
You 'aven't got no brothers, fathers, sisters, wives,or
        sons –
If you want to win your battles take an' work your
        bloomin' guns!

              ' "Snarleyow" ', *BRB*

Yes, makin' mock o' uniforms that guard you while you
        sleep
Is cheaper than them uniforms, an' they're starvation
        cheap ...
    Then it's Tommy this, an' Tommy that, an' 'Tommy,
        'ow's yer soul?'
    But it's 'Thin red line of 'eroes' when the drums begin
        to roll –
    The drums begin to roll, my boys, the drums begin to
        roll,
    O it's 'Thin red line of 'eroes' when the drums begin
        to roll.

We ain't no thin red 'eroes, nor we aren't no blackguards
        too,
But single men in barracks, most remarkable like you ...

You talk o' better food for us, an' schools, an' fires, an'
    all:
We'll wait for extry rations if you treat us rational.
Don't mess about the cook-room slops, but prove it to
    our face
The Widow's Uniform is not the soldier-man's disgrace.
    For it's Tommy this, an' Tommy that, an' 'Chuck him
        out, the brute!'
    But it's 'Saviour of 'is country' when the guns begin to
        shoot;
    An' it's Tommy this, an' Tommy that, an' anything
        you please;
    An' Tommy ain't a bloomin' fool – you bet that
        Tommy sees!                                  'Tommy', *BRB*


You may talk o' gin and beer
When you're quartered safe out 'ere,
An' you're sent to penny-fights an' Aldershot it;
But when it comes to slaughter
You will do your work on water,
An' you'll lick the bloomin' boots of 'im that's got it ...
                                            'Gunga Din', *BRB*


An' for all 'is dirty 'ide
'E was white, clear white, inside
When 'e went to tend the wounded under fire! ...

    Though I've belted you and flayed you,
    By the livin' Gawd that made you,
You're a better man than I am, Gunga Din!            *Ibid*


Then 'ere's *to* you, Fuzzy-Wuzzy, an' the missis and the
        kid;
Our orders was to break you, an' of course we went an'
        did.
We sloshed you with Martinis, an' it wasn't 'ardly fair;
But for all the odds agin' you, Fuzzy-Wuz, you broke the
        square. ...

So 'ere's *to* you, Fuzzy-Wuzzy, at your home in the
      Soudan;
You're a pore benighted 'eathen but a first-class fightin'
      man;
An' 'ere's *to* you, Fuzzy-Wuzzy, with your 'ayrick 'ead
      of 'air –
You big black boundin' beggar – for you broke a British
      square!

                  ' "Fuzzy-Wuzzy" ', *BRB*


Ship me somewheres east of Suez, where the best is like
      the worst,
Where there aren't no Ten Commandments an' a man
      can raise a thirst;
For the temple-bells are callin', an' it's there that I would
      be –
By the old Moulmein Pagoda, looking lazy at the sea;
   On the road to Mandalay,
   Where the old Flotilla lay,
   With our sick beneath the awnings when we went to
      Mandalay!
   O the road to Mandalay,
   Where the flyin'-fishes play,
   An' the dawn comes up like thunder outer China
      'crost the Bay!

                  'Mandalay', *BRB*


We was rotten 'fore we started – we was never
      disci*plined*;
   We made it out a favour if an order was obeyed.
Yes, every little drummer 'ad 'is rights an' wrongs to
      mind,
   So we had to pay for teachin' – an' we paid!

                  'That Day', *SS*


We're most of us liars, we're 'arf of us thieves, an' the
      rest are as rank as can be,
But once in a while we can finish in style (which I 'ope it
      won't 'appen to me).

            ' "Soldier an' Sailor Too" ', *SS*

So it's knock out your pipes an' follow me!
An' it's finish up your swipes an' follow me!
　　Oh, 'ark to the fifes a-crawling!
　　　　Follow me – follow me 'ome!

Take 'im away! 'E's gone where the best men go.
Take 'im away! An' the gun-wheels turnin' slow.
Take 'im away! There's more from the place 'e come.
Take 'im away, with the limber an' the drum.

For it's 'Three rounds blank' an' follow me,
An' it's 'Thirteen rank' an' follow me;
　　Oh, passin' the love o' women,
　　　　Follow me – follow me 'ome!
　　　　　　　　　　　' "Follow Me 'Ome" ', *SS*


When you've shouted 'Rule Britannia', when you've
　　　　sung 'God Save the Queen',
　　When you've finished killing Kruger with your
　　　　mouth,
Will you kindly drop a penny in my little tambourine
　　For a gentleman in khaki ordered South?
He's an absent-minded beggar, and his weaknesses are
　　　　great –
　　But we and Paul must take him as we find him –
He is out on active service, wiping something off a slate –
　　And he's left a lot of little things behind him! ...

There are girls he married secret, asking no permission
　　　　to,
　　For he knew he wouldn't get it if he did.
There is gas and coals and vittles, and the house-rent
　　　　falling due,
　　And it's more than rather likely there's a kid.
There are girls he walked with casual. They'll be sorry
　　　　now he's gone,
　　For an absent-minded beggar they will find him,
But it ain't the time for sermons with the winter coming
　　　　on.
　　We must help the girl that Tommy's left behind him!
　　　　　　　　　'The Absent-Minded Beggar',
　　　　　　　　　*Verse: Inclusive Edition*, 1919

We're foot – slog – slog – slog – sloggin' over Africa –
Foot – foot – foot – foot – sloggin' over Africa –
(Boots – boots – boots – boots – movin' up and down
        again!)
    There's no discharge in the war!

'Boots (*Infantry Columns*)', *FN*


That is what we are known as – we are the beggars that
        got
Three days 'to learn equitation', an' sixth month o'
        bloomin' well trot! ...
But our words o' command are 'Scatter' an' 'Close' an'
        'Let your wounded lie'.
    We used to rescue 'em noble once, –
    Givin' the range as we raised 'em once –
    Gettin' 'em killed as we saved 'em once –
        But now we are M.I. ...


I wish myself could talk to myself as I left 'im a year ago;
I could tell 'im a lot that would save 'im a lot on the
        things that 'e ought to know!
When I think o' that ignorant barrack-bird, it almost
        makes me cry.
    I used to belong in an Army once
    (Gawd! what a rum little Army once),
    Red little, dead little Army once!
        But now I am M.I.!

'M.I. (*Mounted Infantry of the Line*)', *FN*


And it all goes into the laundry,
But it never comes out in the wash,
'Ow we're sugared about by the old men
('Eavy-sterned amateur old men!)
That 'amper an' 'inder an' scold men
For fear o' Stellenbosch!

'Stellenbosch' [where 'the more notoriously incompetent
        commanders used to be sent' in the Boer War], *FN*


Our own utter carelessness, officialdom and ignorance
were responsible for much of the death-rate ... The most
important medical office in any Battalion ought to be
Provost-Marshal of Latrines.

*Something of Myself*, p. 155

They shall not return to us, the resolute, the young,
  The eager and whole-hearted whom we gave:
But the men who left them thriftily to die in their own
      dung,
  Shall they come with years and honour to the grave? ...

Their lives can not repay us – their death could not undo –
  The shame that they have laid upon our race.
But the slothfulness that wasted and the arrogance that
      slew,
  Shall we leave it unabated in its place?
                                'Mesopotamia 1917', *YB*


Pity not! The Army gave
Freedom to a timid slave:
In which Freedom did he find
Strength of body, will, and mind:
By which strength he came to prove
Mirth, Companionship, and Love:
For which Love to Death he went:
In which Death he lies content.
          'Epitaphs of the War 1914-18: Ex-Clerk', *YB*


I could not look on Death, which being known,
Men led me to him, blindfold and alone.
                              *Ibid*: 'The Coward'

If any mourn us in the workshop, say
We died because the shift kept holiday.
                    *Ibid*: 'Batteries out of Ammunition'

If any question why we died,
Tell them, because our fathers lied.
                              *Ibid*: 'Common Form'

I could not dig; I dared not rob:
Therefore I lied to please the mob.
Now all my lies are proved untrue
And I must face the men I slew.
What tale shall serve me here among
Mine angry and defrauded young?
                          *Ibid*: 'A Dead Statesman'

# Lesser Breeds

### Russians

Let is be clearly understood that the Russian is a
delightful person till he tucks in his shirt. As an Oriental
he is charming. It is only when he insists upon being
treated as the most easternly of western peoples instead
of the most westerly of easterns that he becomes a racial
anomaly extremely difficult to handle.

'The Man Who Was', *Life's Handicap*


'Horrible, hairy, human, with paws like hands in prayer,
Making his supplication rose Adam-zad the Bear!
I looked at the swaying shoulders, at the paunch's swag
and swing,
And my heart was touched with pity for the monstrous
pleading thing.

Touched with wonder and pity, I did not fire then ...
I have looked no more on women – I have walked no
more with men.
Nearer he tottered and nearer, with paws like hands that
pray –
From brow to jaw that steel-shod paw, it ripped my face
away! ...

Rouse him at noon in the bushes, follow and press him
hard –
Not for his ragings and roarings flinch ye from
Adam-zad.

But (pay, and I put back the bandage) *this* is the time to
       fear,
When he stands up like a tired man, tottering near and
       near;
When he stands up as pleading, in wavering, man-brute
       guise,
When he veils the hate and cunning of his little swinish
       eyes;

When he shows as seeking quarter, with paws like
       hands in prayer,
*That* is the time of peril – the time of the Truce of the
       Bear!'            'The Truce of the Bear', *FN*


God rest you, thoughtful gentlemen, and send your
       sleep is light!
Remains of this dominion no shadow, sound, or sight,
Except the sound of weeping and the sight of burning
       fire,
And the shadow of a people that is trampled into mire.
    Singing: – Break bread for a starving folk
    That perish in the field.
    Give them their food as they take the yoke ...
    And who shall be next to yield, good sirs,
    For such a bribe to yield?
            'Russia to the Pacifists 1918', *YB*


Even a normal world might become confusing on these
terms, and ours is far from normal. One-sixth of its area
has passed bodily out of civilisation ...
            'Independence', *A Book of Words*, p. 239


But once in a while something happens at sea to remind
us that a ship can be lost in a few hours. And, on land,
we have seen all the Russias – one-sixth of the land-area
of the globe – drive under in a few years.
            'Shipping', *A Book of Words*, p. 268

### Germans

Coldly they went about to raise
   To life and make more dread
Abominations of old days,
   That men believed were dead.

They paid the price to reach their goal
   Across a world in flame;
But their own hate slew their own soul
   Before that victory came.

'The Outlaws', *YB*

Once more we hear the word
That sickened earth of old: –
'No law except the Sword
Unsheathed and uncontrolled.'
Once more it knits mankind,
Once more the nations go
To meet and break and bind
A crazed and driven foe.

' "For All We Have and Are" ', *YB*

… in France and in England, which together compose
the twin fortresses of European civilisation of today, our
folk-tales prefigure our racial temperaments. Every race
betrays itself thus in the tales it tells to its own children.
Let us examine elsewhere. From the earliest ages comes
down to us from out of the North, inhabited by the
tribes of the Teuton and the Tartar, a mass of legend and
story, … which deals with the Wehr-Wolf – the beast
that can at pleasure or for profit change itself into the
likeness of a man and for pleasure or profit become
again the Wolf …
I confess that when I first read them I was fascinated by
the cold tenacity and the ruthlessness of the
Wehr-Wolves, as much as I despised the stupidity of
their victims. For in those days I believed, with the rest
of the world, that such tales came out of the twilight of
primitive savagery. I did not know then, as you and I
know now, that they were the dawn and the forecast of a

modern philosophy of Absolute Evil which has since
been made plain in the face of all mankind.

'A Thesis', *A Book of Words*, pp. 202-4

### Americans

Now this is the Law of the Muscovite, that he proves
        with shot and steel,
When you come by his isles in the Smoky Sea you must
        not take the seal ...
But since our women must walk gay and money buys
        their gear,
The sealing-boats they filch that way at hazard year by
        year.
English they be and Japanee that hang on the Brown
        Bear's flank,
And some be Scot, but the worst of the lot, and the
        boldest thieves, be Yank!

'The Rhyme of the Three Sealers', *SS*

Let there be no misunderstanding about the matter. I
love this People, and if any contemptuous criticism has
to be done, I will do it myself ... They are bleeding-raw
at the edges, almost more conceited than the English,
vulgar with a massive vulgarity which is as though the
Pyramids were coated with Christmas-cake
sugar-works. Cocksure they are, lawless and as casual as
they are cocksure; but I love them, and I realised it when
I met an Englishman who laughed at them ...

*From Sea to Sea*, Vol. II, p. 130

There is nothing known to man that [the American of
the Future] will not be, and his country will sway the
world with one foot as a man tilts a see-saw plank! ...
You wait and see. Sixty million people, chiefly of English
instincts, who are trained from youth to believe that
nothing is impossible, don't slink through the centuries
like Russian peasantry. They are bound to leave their
mark somewhere, and don't you forget it.

*Ibid*, pp. 131-2

Every nation, like every individual, walks in a vain show – else it could not live with itself – but I never got over the wonder of a people who, having extirpated the aboriginals of their continent more completely than any modern race had ever done, honestly believed that they were a godly little New England community, setting examples to brutal mankind. *Something of Myself*, p. 123

I wanted to see if I could catch and hold something of a rather beautiful localised American atmosphere that was already beginning to fade.

*Ibid*, p. 131 (on *Captains Courageous*)

It was then that I first began to wonder whether Abraham Lincoln had not killed rather too many autochthonous 'Americans' in the Civil War, for the benefit of their hastily imported Continental supplanters ...
*Ibid*, p. 128

They were an interesting folk, but behind their desperate activities lay always, it seemed to me, immense and unacknowledged boredom – the deadweight of material things passionately worked up into Gods, that only bored their worshippers more and worse and longer.
*Ibid*, p. 132

And always the marvel – to which the Canadians seemed insensible – was that on one side of an imaginary line should be Safety, Law, Honour, and Obedience, and on the other frank, brutal decivilisation, and that, despite this, Canada should be impressed by any aspect whatever of the United States. *Ibid*, p. 200

Brethren, how shall it fare with me
    When the war is laid aside,
If it be proven that I am he
    For whom a world has died?

If it be proven that all my good,
    And the greater good I will make,
Were purchased me by a multitude
    Who suffered for my sake?
'The Question' '(Attitude of the United States of America during the first two years, seven months and four days of the Great War)', *YB*

# Wise Saws & Modern Instances

I keep six honest serving-men
   (They taught me all I knew);
Their names are What and Why and When
   And How and Where and Who.
Just So Stories ('The Elephant's Child')

Children tell little more than animals, for what comes to
them they accept as eternally established. Also,
badly-treated children have a clear notion of what they
are likely to get if they betray the secrets of a
prison-house before they are clear of it.
Something of Myself, p. 15

One learns more from a good scholar in a rage than from
a score of lucid and laborious drudges.
Ibid, p. 32

The toad beneath the harrow knows
Exactly where each tooth-point goes;
The butterfly upon the road
Preaches contentment to that toad.
'Pagett, M.P.', DD

Pleasant it is for the Little Tin Gods
   When great Jove nods;
But Little Tin Gods make their little mistakes
In missing the hour when great Jove wakes.
Heading, 'A Germ-Destroyer', Plain Tales

'Stopped in the straight when the race was his own!
Look at him cutting it – cur to the bone!'
Ask, ere the youngster be rated and chidden,
What did he carry and how was he ridden?
Maybe they used him too much at the start.
Maybe Fate's weight-cloths are breaking his heart.
Heading, 'In the Pride of his Youth', Plain Tales

Ride with an idle whip, ride with an unused heel,
But, once in a way, there will come a day
When the colt must be taught to feel
The lash that falls, and the curb that galls, and the sting
of the rowelled steel.

Heading, 'The Conversion of Aurelian McGoggin', *Plain Tales*

'And some are sulky, while some will plunge.
(*So ho! Steady! Stand still, you!*)
Some you must gentle, and some you must lunge,
(*There! There! Who wants to kill you?*)
Some – there are losses in every trade –
Will break their hearts ere bitted and made,
Will fight like fiends as the rope cuts hard,
And die dumb-mad in the breaking yard.'

Heading, 'Thrown Away', *Plain Tales*

If He play, being young and unskilful, for shekels of
silver and gold,
Take His money, my son, praising Allah. The kid was
ordained to be sold.

'Certain Maxims of Hafiz', *DD*

A stone's throw out on either hand
From that well-ordered road we tread,
And all the world is wild and strange …

Heading, 'In the House of Suddhoo', *Plain Tales*

Still the world is wondrous large, – seven seas from
marge to marge –
And it holds a vast of various kinds of man;
And the wildest dreams of Kew are the facts of
Khatmandhu.
And the crimes of Clapham chaste in Martaban.

'In the Neolithic Age', *SS*

My brother kneels, so saith Kabir,
To stone and brass in heathen wise,
But in my brother's voice I hear
My own unanswered agonies.
His God is as his fates assign,
His prayer is all the world's – and mine.

'The Prayer', Chapter Heading, *Kim*

They're all awa'! True beat, full power, the clangin'
        chorus goes
Clear to the tunnel where they sit, my purrin' dynamoes.
Interdependence absolute, foreseen, ordained, decreed,
To work, Ye'll note, at ony tilt an' every rate o' speed ...
Now, a' together, hear them lift their lesson – theirs an'
        mine:
'Law, Orrder, Duty an' Restraint, Obedience, Discipline!'
                        'McAndrew's Hymn', *SS*


And they asked me how I did it, and I gave 'em the
        Scripture text,
'You keep your light so shining a little in front o' the
        next!'
They copied all they could follow, but they couldn't
        copy my mind,
And I left 'em sweating an' stealing a year and a half
        behind ...

Harrer an' Trinity College! I ought to ha' sent you to sea –
But I stood you an education, an' what have you done
        for me?
The things I knew was proper you wouldn't thank me to
        give,
And the things I knew was rotten you said was the way
        to live.
For you muddled with books and pictures, an' china an'
        etchin's an' fans,
And your rooms at college was beastly – more like a
        whore's than a man's;
Till you married that thin-flanked woman, as white and
        as stale as a bone,
An' she gave you your social nonsense; but where's that
        kid o' your own?
I've seen your carriages blocking the half o' the
        Cromwell Road,
But never the doctor's brougham to help the missus
        unload ...

Never seen death yet, Dickie? ... Well, now is your time
        to learn!
                      'The "Mary Gloster"', *SS*

'I like men who do things.'

> The heroine in 'William the Conqueror',
> *The Day's Work*

From forge and farm and mine and bench,
    Deck, altar, outpost lone –
Mill, school, battalion, counter, trench,
    Rail, senate, sheepfold, throne –
Creation's cry goes up on high
    From age to cheated age:
'Send us the men who do the work
    For which they draw the wage!'

> 'The Wage-Slaves', *FN*

Our fathers they left us their blessing –
    They taught us and groomed us and crammed;
But we've shaken the Clubs and the Messes
    To go and find out and be damned
                        (Dear boys!),
    To go and get shot and be damned.

> 'The Lost Legion', *SS*

We have done with Hope and Honour, we are lost to
                        Love and Truth,
    We are dropping down the ladder rung by rung,
And the measure of our torment is the measure of our
                        youth.
    God help us, for we knew the worst too young!

> 'Gentlemen-Rankers', *BRB*

Here I come to my own again,
Fed, forgiven and known again,
Claimed by bone of my bone again
And cheered by flesh of my flesh.
The fatted calf is dressed for me,
But the husks have greater zest for me.
I think my pigs will be best for me,
So I'm off to the Yards afresh.

I never was very refined, you see,
(And it weighs on my brother's mind, you see)
But there's no reproach among swine, d'you see,
For being a bit of a swine …

So I was a mark for plunder at once,
And lost my cash (can you wonder?) at once,
But I didn't give up and knock under at once.
I worked in the Yards for a spell,
Where I spent my nights and my days with hogs,
And shared their milk and maize with hogs,
Till, I guess, I have learned what pays with hogs
And – I have that knowledge to sell!
> 'The Prodigal Son (Western Version)' (enlarged
> from Chapter Heading, *Kim*)


Try as he will, no man breaks wholly loose
    From his first love, no matter who she be.
Oh, was there ever sailor free to choose,
    That didn't settle somewhere near the sea? …

*Parsons in pulpits, tax-payers in pews,*
    *Kings on your thrones, you know as well as me,*
*We've only one virginity to lose,*
    *And where we lost it there our hearts will be!*
> 'The Virginity', *YB*


If you wake at midnight, and hear a horse's feet,
Don't go drawing back the blind, or looking in the street,
Them that asks no questions isn't told a lie.
Watch the wall, my darling, while the Gentlemen go by!
> 'A Smuggler's Song', *Puck*


It is always a temptation to a rich and lazy nation,
    To puff and look important and to say: –
'Though we know we should defeat you, we have not
            the time to meet you.
We will therefore pay you cash to go away.'

And that is called paying the Dane-geld;
    But we've proved it again and again,
That if once you have paid him the Dane-geld
    You never get rid of the Dane.
> 'Dane-Geld (A.D. 980-1016)', *School History*

If you can keep your head when all about you
  Are losing theirs and blaming it on you,
If you can trust yourself when all men doubt you,
  But make allowance for their doubting too;
If you can wait and not be tired by waiting,
  Or being lied about, don't deal in lies,
Or being hated, don't give way to hating,
  And yet don't look too good, nor talk too wise:


If you can dream – and not make dreams your master;
  If you can think – and not make thoughts your aim;
If you can meet with Triumph and Disaster
  And treat those two imposters just the same;
If you can bear to hear the truth you've spoken
  Twisted by knaves to make a trap for fools,
Or watch the things you gave your life to, broken,
  And stoop and build 'em up with worn-out tools:


If you can make one heap of all your winnings
  And risk it on one turn of pitch-and-toss,
And lose, and start again at your beginnings
  And never breathe a word about your loss;
If you can force your heart and nerve and sinew
  To serve your turn long after they are gone,
And so hold on when there is nothing in you
  Except the Will which says to them: 'Hold on!'


If you can talk with crowds and keep your virtue,
  Or walk with Kings – nor lose the common touch,
If neither foes nor loving friends can hurt you,
  If all men count with you, but none too much;
If you can fill the unforgiving minute
  With sixty seconds' worth of distance run,
Yours is the Earth and everything that's in it,
  And – which is more – you'll be a Man, my son!
                                        'If –', *Rewards and Fairies*

Read here the moral roundly writ
    For him who into battle goes –
Each soul that, hitting hard or hit,
    Endureth gross or ghostly foes.
    Prince, blown by many overthrows,
Half blind with shame, half choked with dirt,
    *Man cannot tell, but Allah knows*
*How much the other side was hurt!*

> 'Verses on Games: Boxing', *Almanac of Twelve
> Sports, 1898* (William Nicholson)


Now this is the Law of the Jungle – as old and as true as
        the sky;
And the Wolf that shall keep it may prosper, but the
        Wolf that shall break it must die.

As the creeper that girdles the tree-trunk the Law
        runneth forward and back –
For the strength of the Pack is the Wolf, and the strength
        of the Wolf is the Pack.

> 'The Law of the Jungle', *The Second
> Jungle Book* ('How Fear Came')


Thus it happened, but none can tell
What was the Power behind the spell –
Fear, or Duty, or Pride, or Faith –
That sent men shuddering out to death –
To cold and watching, and, worse than these,
Work, more work, when they looked for ease –
To the day's discomfort, the night's despair,
In the hope of a prize that they never could share.

(Singing) *'Eenee, Meenee, Mainee, Mo!*
*Man is born to Toil and Woe.*
*One will cure the other – so*
*Eenee, Meenee, Mainee, Mo*
*Make – You – It.'* ...

Nothing is left of that terrible rune
But a tag of gibberish tacked to a tune
That ends the waiting and settles the claims
Of children arguing over their games ...

> 'A Counting-Out Song', *Land and Sea Tales
> for Scouts and Guides*

Files –
The Files –
Office Files!
Oblige me by referring to the Files.
Every question man can raise,
Every phrase of every phase
Of that question is on record in the Files –
(Threshed out threadbare – fought and finished in the
                  Files).                              'The Files', *FN*


As I pass through my incarnations in every age and race,
I make my proper prostrations to the Gods of the
                  Market-Place.
Peering through reverent fingers I watch them flourish
                  and fall,
And the Gods of the Copybook Headings, I notice,
                  outlast them all.


We were living in trees when they met us. They showed
                  us each in turn
That Water would certainly wet us, as Fire would
                  certainly burn:
But we found them lacking in Uplift, Vision and Breadth
                  of Mind,
So we left them to teach the Gorillas while we followed
                  the March of Mankind …


With the Hopes that our World is built on they were
                  utterly out of touch,
They denied that the Moon was Stilton; they denied she
                  was even Dutch.
They denied that Wishes were Horses; they denied that
                  a Pig had Wings.
So we worshipped the Gods of the Market who
                  promised these beautiful things …


In the Carboniferous Epoch we were promised
                  abundance for all,
By robbing selected Peter to pay for collective Paul;
But, though we had plenty of money, there was nothing
                  our money could buy,
And the Gods of the Copybook Headings said: '*If you
                  don't work you die.*' …

As it will be in the future, it was at the birth of Man –
There are only four things certain since Social Progress
         began: –
That the Dog returns to his Vomit and the Sow returns
         to her Mire,
And the burnt Fool's bandaged finger goes wabbling
         back to the Fire;

And that after this is accomplished, and the brave new
         world begins
When all men are paid for existing and no man must
         pay for his sins,
As surely as Water will wet us, as surely as Fire will burn,
The Gods of the Copybook Headings with terror and
         slaughter return!
> 'The Gods of the Copybook Headings (1919)',
> *Verse, Inclusive Edition*, 1927


We know that Ones and Ones make Twos –
    Till Demos votes them Three or Nought.
We know the Fenris Wolf is loose.
    We know what Fight has not been fought.
    We know the Father to the Thought
Which argues Babe and Cockatrice
    Would play together, were they taught.
We know *that* Bonfire on the Ice.

We know that Thriving comes by Thrift.
    We know the Key must keep the Door.
We know his Boot-straps cannot lift
    The frightened Waster off the floor.
    We know these things, and we deplore
That not by any Artifice
    Can they be altered. Furthermore
    We know the Bonfires on the Ice!
> 'The Bonfires (1933)' '("*Gesture … outlook … vision … avenue*
> *… example … achievement … appeasement … limit of risk*" –
> Common Political Form)', DE

The careful text-books measure
  (Let all who build beware!)
The load, the shock, the pressure
  Material can bear.
So, when the buckled girder
  Lets down the grinding span,
The blame of loss, or murder,
  Is laid upon the man.
      *Not on the stuff – the Man!*

But, in our daily dealing
  With stone and steel, we find
The Gods have no such feeling
  Of justice toward mankind.
To no set gauge they make us, –
  For no laid course prepare –
And presently o'ertake us
  With loads we cannot bear:
      *Too merciless to bear.*

'Hymn of Breaking Strain', *DE*

A veil 'twixt us and Thee, Good Lord,
A veil 'twixt us and Thee –
Lest we should hear too clear, too clear,
And unto madness see!

'The Prayer of Miriam Cohen', from Heading in
*Many Inventions* ('The Disturber of Traffic')